MUSE

THE LOVE AND ROMANCE

MITHUN PRAKASH

For you

Contents

Contents

Contents

Contents

Contents

Contents

Contents

Contents

Contents

Contents

Author

Mithun Prakash was a young writer and film student. His debut Tamil book "Ayan imayam thotta thirai iyakunarkal"

It showcased the myriad variations of cinema, art, and passionate filmmakers and their formidable creations.

His writing revolves around the themes of dreams, hope, courage, friendship, love, and his beautiful world to fill his readers with positivity and happiness.

Preface

I was going through the romantic poets, looking for a quote to head this little introduction, but somehow the right sentiments eluded me. It must have been years ago. I was 8 when I first fell in love. We were in grade 4 in the section 'A'. One Day in a drawing class, I was trying to draw a blue butterfly. Catastrophe struck when in an exaggerated effort to color within the wings, I broke the tip of my blue pencil. My cartoon-themed ben ten sharpener refused to work. And all of a sudden the tip of my nose had turned red; tears threatened to spill over my half-painted masterpiece. Seeing my sad face, a long-haired little girl reached out and offered her sole blue crayon. We exchanged a gummy smile, and at that moment, I was introduced to the elation of love.

I have searched for the perfect words to capture what love can mean. The magic of first sight, the high feeling of a first crush, to glancing at your watch every five minutes, waiting impatiently for your date to arrive. the sunken feeling of rejection, the sky-high exuberance of emerging from pain like a butterfly.

Falling in love and heartbreak is probably the best thing that can happen to people. It gives a certain spontaneity and intensity. Whether it strikes one at first sight or blooms gradually, people cannot help falling in love and then writing about it. Love poems have been written for centuries. Message captured by readers as the impression after reading the poem. How the reader concludes poetry is closely related to the point of view of the reader toward something.

The very image of the people sitting with pen in hand, brooding and pining for their love while composing heartfelt lines, evokes elegance. The season of Light, the season of Darkness, the wisdom, the foolishness, the epoch of belief, the epoch of incredulity, the spring of hope, the winter of despair. It is an indefinable, infinite emotion. Perhaps the most powerful of feelings, it can be beautiful, painful, and at times, all - consuming and dangerous. indescribable nature is what makes it both the thing we long for and the thing that torments us. We've all been there. It's no surprise that the various dimensions of love have inspired artists and cultures around the world.

Muse is weaving through the expanse of emotions that make up love, within these pages you may find yourself reliving many familiar, bittersweet, and uplifting moments.

Conquer them with butterflies and muse.

Lots of love with

Mithun prakash

Email : imithunprakash@gmail.com

Instagaram : @imithunprakash

1. Begins

Where dark ends, love begins.
Where love ends, poetry begins.

2. Intuition

Poetry is the starting point of an intuition
Intuition is the starting point of a poetry

3. Unanswerable

You are asking me for the most beautiful poetry,
I know nothing beyond the first word of this.

4. insect

Love is a butterfly
Nectar-feeding insect,
With two pairs of large
Brightly colored wings.

5. Wolf in myself

Once I saw her
Leaning over the balcony railing
she has a full moon in her eyes
so I look at her with
wolf in myself
Her cold and brazen attitude
Sends shivers
She's a hunter made for
The Wild
My cupid's arrows
Don't work on
Girl with guns.

6. in my mind

Among the mob
I search to meet her gaze,
But get lost in her serenity.
Her innocent smiles
And when she looks at me
I swear I can't breathe.
What happened to me?
I feel
Butterflies fluttered in my mind.

7. way back home

Moon,
I am far from my whereabouts
as I stare into your eyes
which are a mellow sunset,
I forget my fear
of the ominous dark night that
follows,
which is your love
and as the crepuscular rays
vanish into the darkness
so do my hopes
of finding my way back home.

8. chaos theory

I'm lying down on the terrace
My glimpse at the sky
I told the moon that I saw a brighter
Moon than you
I told the stars that
lass's smile is more
beautiful than
You…
when the sky sees me
it's chaos theory.

9. The ocean

From the clouds
We're like two drops of water
Flowing In different rivers,
Hoping to mix in the ocean.

10. Snooze

I always snooze the alarms
that Woke me up from our
memories,
The blaze of sunshine
touches my face
as I woke up with your thoughts
I can't erase it.
and then outside the window,
the view I start to gaze at;
trying to solve the mystery
as complex as a maze.

11. Ernest hemingway

A cat in the rain,
The sea broke in a long line
in the rain and slipped back
down the beach to come up
a break again in long in the rain.

12. Begs for attention

The moon
and the breeze
and rain is behind him
and the moon
and the breeze
and rain is in front of him,
The moon never begs for attention.

13. A herb of healing

The muse in boyhood.
I walked alone and thought.
The wild brown woods among,
Where the roads part them hurry,
And so the weed of sorrow Springs
at the four crossways.
By night I plucked it hueless,
It seemed a herb of healing
I would seek and find.

14. He hopes

She was sitting in a window one day,
gazing, how the wind holds the trees
in its hands, helping them to sway
when he walked through
the same street,
He hopes one day he will
catch a spark in her spirit again
and burn in the way she desires,
and not go down in someone
else's flames again.

15. where

You are living
and breathing
"somewhere far away,"
"quite close to me,"
"inside myself."

16. She's looking

Not paying attention to much of anything.
She is coming in,
Her smile melts me.
"Hi," I finally manage to say,
she waves and then walks away.
Lowly, all feeling comes back to me,
Hi? I think to myself,
angered that I hadn't said more
and hadn't kept her longer.
Later in the cafe,
I can't help but steal a glance at her,
she's looking at me too!
I quickly turn back to this page.

17. What

As yet unknown
What makes your face Distinctive.

18. the first time

In candlelight a chamber,
Shall we fall in love
with each other
Over and over
For the first time
Just one more time?

19. Enticing dessert

In post supper
She looks like sugar,
Smells like coco
Mocha almond fudge
On top of chocolate lava
Her luring eyes tell me
She's an enticing dessert
Fantasy

20. Violence

Violence is peace
Her heart's scream rose
Even though her outer silence
With her alluring eyes
She flaunted a strong Passion.
And through her emotions
She held love and lust in a balance
But her type of romance
was suffused with lethal
Violence.

21. Greedy person

You are a treasure trove
Is it wrong to be a greedy person?

22. Corner of your lips

The flames you see in my heart
is but a reflection
of the spark
I saw in your eyes,
Why does my gaze turn
At every corner of your lips
when you blush?

23. Swallow my pride

While lips drenched
I had to swallow my pride
When you chewed my heart
to bits and pieces.

24. Fight for Space

Night sky
and silent road
I dream of long walks
in the Rain,
Where we playfully
fight for Space
Under an umbrella
And I hold onto your hand to
Show you
That you're safe in this storm

25. Under her Eyes

I read her gaze
those black lines
under her Eyes
will always be more
beautiful than
all the poetic lines I will
ever write
about them.

26. Harmony

She speaks music in eloquent Sonnets
her voice is a sonorous harmony
composed by A. R. Rahman
but I'm stuck in the first

stanza.

27. Void in my heart

Muse,
Before I met your glimpse
I felt that I couldn't love anyone,
that nobody would be able to
fill the void in my heart,
but that all changed
when I met your gaze
then I came to realize
you were always on my mind
you were my pillar
when I was falling
you were my strength
when I felt low with your smile,
You make me weak
when I talk to you
then I started to write
poems about you.

28. I wake

On your laps
If I die before I wake,
It's because you take
my breath away,

29. I Love you

I Love you as you lay
a kiss upon my lips,
as the heart in my chest flips
I Love you as
a bee loves its honey,
as an angel loves her wings
I Love you as
a fish loves the sea,
how the bird loves to sing
I love you and hold you tight
as you tell me everything is all right.

30. Where

Where in your body can I find love...?
It's in the place where my hand has never touched it.

31. Venom we call love

Kiss me with venom
that venom we call love
venom each other purity
like two dying doves
and let's rise like a
pair of phoenix.

32. A rope

With a rope of our bodies
my soul is connected to yours
all of our ambitions were tied to it
my fold flesh cries out for more
no matter how long I keep
my lips pressed against on you.

33. It was

A sugary fluid secreted,
within ourselves to encourage pollination by love.

34. Definition

Love is,
a colorless, transparent,
the odorless liquid
that forms the rain,
lakes, rivers, and seas and is
the basis of the fluids of
living organisms.

35. The rhythm

Sleep only wakes me up at night.
there's something quieter than sleep within this inner room!
the rhythm which projects from itself
continuity bending all to its force
from window to door,
from ceiling to floor,
the light at the opening,
dark at the closing.

36. On armless chair

Our hands seek each other out,
two little birds nesting close,
not making a sound but
bursting with a song.

37. The other way

From across this quiet garden,
the butterfly told me
I should abandon this poem,
should leave these words to the diary,
rise from this lawn and come to conscious
the state of being awake,
another might look the other way,
obey the intuition muse
and keep the poem going.

38. Stories to be told

Tales we never wrote
I hope someday we learn
to look past our eyes
and into our souls
as our timing together files,
and as we turn beautifully old
let's create memories
and many lovely stories to be
told.

39. Diagnosis

Your melancholy
is the ink I use
to write a prescription
to your soul.

40. Stupor

The thirst to burn the world,
moonlight and romantic
walks in the rain
will never describe
our love's Flame
that thirst to burn the world
around us in a stupor
our abomination is fascination.

41. Love your

I love your eyes
when the lovelight lies
lit with a passionate fire
I love your arms
when the warm white flesh
touches mine in a fond embrace
I love your hair
when the strands enmesh
your kisses on my face.

42. Expecting

Kiss sometimes when no one is looking,

43. Herself is the remedy

Disease and medicine
To the pain she gives,
herself is the remedy
they whispered
all their flaws
and inhaled
the storm together.

44. In her embrace

whose locks with flowery
wreaths are bound,
each varied form of elation
the soul can wish for is found,
step lightly on the narrow spot
the broadest plant that grows
is not so ample as the breast
these pollen seams encircle.

45. You are

You are my consciousness
I don't know where you are,
You aren't somewhere inside me

"You are me."

46. Losing innocence

The fairy appeared
from the woman
who had stripped
herself naked again that night
losing innocence
as lust creeps in slowly
not In our sense.

47. A painting

Leonardo da Vinci, a painter
who draws with one hand
at the same moment,
writes with another hand
you are a painting,
stroking the hair with one hand
while writing on another hand.

48. I wait only for

I dream of you clothed in white.
you wear wings
that glow with golden light,
your eyes hold a vision of the road of life
you whisper love through the winds
then rivers of love flow to my heart
I grow embraced by heavenly heights,
then glow rays of warmth and light.
I wait only for your touch of the purest.

49. Fails me

If I had the words
to describe my feelings
when you see my eyes
I would be the happiest
man in the universe
But words seem to
fails me again and again

50. The bright blue sky

*The grandiose rainbow etched
in the bright blue sky
can't catch my attention,
when you are passing by.
You are the only one
who fill color into my eyes
and it will be of extreme joy
if you will be with me during the rainfall
under the umbrella.*

51. Solace

Sometimes,
I'm sorrowful and
life gets me down,
I always know
I can turn that around,
by closing my eyes
and picturing you,
the source of my relief.

52. Fall in tune

53. Whenever we're apart

You're a flower in bloom.
In the dark, in the gloom,
butterflies can't find nectar
whenever we're apart.

54. A song of my touch

The beating of your heart
is like a song of my touch,
I never want to spend a minute
without tasting your tongue
the way you kiss me takes
my breath away,

55. Take

Take my heart;
I'll give it with ease.
Take my fears;
make them vanish when things get tough.
Take my scars;
and heal them all up.
Take my smile;
and make it stretch so wide.
Take my hand;
and walk this journey with me.
Take these feelings;
and make them real.
In the end,
show me how to feel.

56. I'm not asleep

I look at the sky,
I see your face in the clouds.
the tree branches Seem to
spell out your name.
the wind always sounds like your voice,
calling me to hug.
you're in my dreams
even though I'm not asleep.

57. Wishing for another chance

You got me writing love songs
no singer can sing
cause you've got me
wrapped up in your silk skin.
You got me writing love songs
to express how much
I missed your touch
wishing for another chance
to embrace and savor the lost times.

58. When words fail

Mouths spoke without words

59. Under your hands all day

If I had myself as
the keyboard, the mouse of
I'd be under your hands all day.
press enter,
and I'll be there.

60. The sensation

A breeze wrapped around
the night was hushed
except for the sound of
two young hearts beating
she leaned down toward me
her gentle lips persuaded mine,
soft and sweet as cotton candy
we savored the sensation
and tasted each other slowly.

61. Beauty's self

Winter, spring,
and summer
for every season
she hath dressings fit,
no beauty she doth miss
when all her robes are on,
but Beauty's self she is
when all her robes are gone.

62. The moonbow

Muse occupation the night,
upon I looked, I listened to the rain
It was an enchanting scene
a multitude of muse
among the moonbow,
cold and blue night,
and then a rope of magic around my body
a long stretch of light shot up at me,
when I awoke
it was already day
I did the same again
watched and listened to the night.

63. kindle

Every kiss provokes another

64. Tips of her fingers

She belligerent on the bowl
as she fights with pasta
with the tips of her fingers
she sees him in a different dimension,
he watches the way she eats
and think better of saying anything.

65. Wink

When she takes him,
in Stars swoon
unborn babes long
to hear their names,
he loses his voice
and has to write it
all down to the diary
she spills a glass of wine
the ink blurs and swims
across the page,
he stared in annoyance
she winked innocently.

66. Another moon

On the pillow,
who could read my speechless mind
I turn to her, holding my breath
she cups my hand against her cheeks
tilt her head and kiss my wrist
taking away all of my concerns
in the light of another moon.

67. Cup of coffee

My camera will tell me
what I did, It will record the
under the table, toes kissing each other
the walkthrough streets,
the corner café, and the moment.
A camera will tell me
what I did not do or say
It will tell me
you were not in the frame
It will show me the streets
you haven't walked in
It will show me
an empty chair, your cup of
coffee is untouched.

68. Hold my breath

All night,
my face next to your chest,
I hold my breath,
listening to yours
your dreams are a trapeze faces
lift like mirrored moons
hung above your sleep,
a circus of stars.

69. My name

I love my name
When you whisper it.

70. God went to her house

A sobbing fish in a bowl i was,
a bottom feeder,
but now I nurse
upon abreast in the sky
god went to her house
and asked for charity,
she fell to her knees and cried,
"Adored, what may I give?" she asked.
"Just love," He said.

71. Promises

Eyes closed,
Yet we saw deeply into each other's self and essence
Unspoken promises filled us with dreams of our tomorrow
that we remember today.

72. Books on bed

She prefers,
a quiet walk along the shore
dinner with red wine
duet in candlelight
movies with a melancholic touch
Jane Austen's books on bed
melodies in moonlight
the scent of his chest.

73. I know

A pin-drop silence In the library
before he can speak,
she leans between the shelf,
fingers barely touching
the corner of his mouth,
already I know, he said.

74. Corner seat

In the darkness
of the theatre,
I leaned over
and found her lips
our double-headed silhouette
against the screen
and clashed.

75. Custard

A naked tight sleep
makes feel like custard
undress in the afternoon
in a room made filled
with dark silence
the curtains only eclipse
the neighbors' view.

76. Yearning

While your face isn't clear,
needing to find,
you are that nothing
when people ask me
what I'm thinking.
while we haven't found
each other yet,
I know you're out there
I just don't know where
I might not have
your permission But,
I will still be at your doorstep
with the yearning of my heart.

77. Own universe

Poets are often those who build their own universe,
Muse and me.

78. Her palm

A state of the skin caused by cold,
fear, longing, or excitement, in which
small bumps appear on the surface
as the hairs become erect, when
her palm touches his chest.

79. Floating

The sun and clouds
they kiss sometimes
a visible mass of condensed
water vapor floating in the atmosphere,
typically high above the ground.

80. Sky

Her umbrella receives countless kisses from the cloud.

81. When a girl grieves

Cannot stop the passion
that surges to life,
heart yearning as it did
the very first time, and want to do
what autumn does to maple leaves,
to use no kind of conciliating art
when a girl grieves, Is cutting out the root
of the tender winding tree that droops.

82. Jasmine

Come slowly,
count his countless,
nectars entering
as the fainting bee,
reaching late his flower,
lips unused to you,
sip your jasmines,
hover her chamber hums,
the lust can break
the door of chastity
which is bolted with modesty.

83. Alive

Stay close to anything
that makes me alive
I hide within a flower,
that fading from your hair,
feel for me Almost a loneliness,
leave scent and traces of myself
where I feel comfortable,
most worthwhile.

84. at night

Love birds
Why are they so shy before us?

85. Naturally,

The kisses spring into bonding
pressed one against another,
until would find it as hard to count
the kisses were exchanged in a minute.

86. The nightly game

Love birds own the day
lust bats own the night
at the break of dawn
both take flight,
until darkness is gone
vampire bats steal our lust blood
empire birds heal our love
want them to stay in their soul
by the nightly game
will shift into bats.

87. Nest

Feathers remark that birds have fled!

88. White water-louts

When at dawn
her fair face gazes
out in the sky
through the window wood
beauteous she looks
like a white water-louts
bursting out of bud on pool
cherish roses peep into
her chamber Jasmine and woodbine
breath sweet, fill her with balm
nested from head to feet.

89. Booze

The boozer soul rise
drink to me only with your gaze
and I will pledge with mine
or leave a kiss on my lip
and I will not look for a booze
but I will look for nectar sup.

90. Blessed

Her eyes were a milky way
when she met my gaze
the beauty of the night stars,
sky and all the wonders
it carries with it
have I been blessed with
my eyes to watch this
fulfilling sight daily.

91. Infant

I hold my pen
to write a journal of my love
pregnant with the incredible ink of our dream,
I'm with little well content
and a little from thee sent
is enough with true intent
her breast was a table
my thoughts were an infant
which would thereon have fed.

92. Rehub

I'm Gathering sticks for the nest

93. Sip

I will garnish us with
mangos and marionberry
sip the juice that drips
so sweet from the heat of the heart
her nipperkin is overflowing.

94. Cat in the rain

I'm not sure if it'll rain or not.
in the land where we do lie,
your wind brings up the rain
cloud between the twain
wide apart lie we,
we isolated together.

95. Stone heart

Her heart was a precious stone
consisting of a clear and
colorless crystalline
form of pure soul.

96. Tangled

The diamond tears adorning
that weeps,
her wounded arm, his damaged toes
haltingly he touched her tarnished neck tenderly
she traces the ridges of his chest scar,
as sweet dreams legs entwined
souls too well tangled.

97. Pull off

An act of holding tightly in arms,
a sign of affection.
I wanted to hug you.

98. Make-believe

She comes to me in dreams at midnight,
her eyes look through me
as her hands caress my face.
her words are as kind
as her laughter is playful.
I love the muse of my heart
and know her not by daybreak.

99. Tomorrow

I lay in bed,
I close my ears to all sounds,
I close my eyes to all sight.
In my mind,
I see her smiling,
Her brown eyes glowing
I make up my mind:
Tomorrow I will tell her how I feel.

100. Mystery

Sometimes,
I don't understand her eyes hint.

101. The corners of nature

It's her name the birds sing
every morning,
her voice that the winds carry
in the warm afternoon,
she's vivid and beautiful
sunset.
and also the effulgent full moon
at midnight.
Why do I find her in all
the corners of nature
that I am Yet to explore.

102. Sprinkle

Odor is around me
let these winds
caress your skin
that they may
evaporate into clouds
and pour your scent
as rain for me.

103. Lustful

I didn't want
only lust
I only wanted something
to end my loneliness,
maybe add rueful life.
I didn't want
only romance
I only wanted someone,
to listen to my grievance,
maybe replace my sorrows
with some lustful romance.

104. Rose between two thorns

My muse,
your lips are soft red rose
that I will carry in my heart.
I'll bathe in your fragrance
and caress your petals.

105. Combust

I think her glimpse
must give off all the heat
I'll ever need it, It's hot
like branding iron
and sweet.
as the weather gets colder
It pulls me in
her warm cozy fire
growing hotter by the minute, hour, day
I may just spontaneously
combust Right here
In her arms.

106. Amalgamation

Link hands and laugh with me

107. On the mattress

As induced by hypnosis or entered by her
a half-conscious state characterized
by an absence of response to external stimuli, dreaming of the
long.
the neighbors hammered on the walls all night,
the next door was outraged by the noise
we made it on the mattress.

108. Gird

I navigated by your fragrance
every route brings me to you,
and every time I gaze into your eyes,
I attempt to discover myself in them
keep me close to your chest
I forgot about the sleep
since I was wrapped in your arms.

109. Disclose

The mist of my breath
slides off the angled mirror to reveal your face

110. Mix paint

An artist mix paint
Brushing her eyes seductress,
On Canvas
Your gaze makes me an artist.

111. Never saw her

There are no volcanoes in India.
I think our geologists never saw her in anger.

112. Words

I've been hiding
behind metaphors
for too long, calling you
the moon, speaking of the sea
dancing in the rain.
when you look at me,
I've been trying to
speak love indirectly,
never understanding
that you only craved my lips and soul
not words.

113. Let

Let us relive the evenings
Let's relive the white nights
Let us go back to that conversation
Let those restless moments revived
Let your heart cry out of pain
Just give me a hug
of the time we spent together.

114. Hunt the heart

In just a moment,
I melted
what's wrong with me?
Your eyes hunt the heart of mine
melt immediately
in just a moment,
I melted.

115. Delicate

Even the thin fold skin
of eyes
speaks a lot
when staring into that
tonguing over and over,
closed Eyelids.

116. Perk

Beneath your dress,
I find Rewarding
to my explorations,
certain, Soft and flowing,
and tender to a touch of love.

117. 2 AM

I entered through
her bedroom window
she hurried at his words,
beset with fears
for there were sleeping
dragons all around,
at a glaring watch, 2 AM
up the wide stairs
a darkling way found
to terrace.

118. Take me there

I have nowhere to go
I follow your fragrance
I keep wandering around
every path leads me to your doorstep
my destination is in your arms
take me there.

119. Faint

You saw my starved lips in the gloam
With horrid warning carried close
unpin that spangled breastplate that you wear
unlace yourself, that harmonious heart
rhythm tells me from you that now is bedtime,
She made me faint asleep
pillowed upon my fairy's ripening breast
to feel forever its soft fall and swell
awake forever in a sweet unrest
still, to hear her tender taken lungs breath
and so live ever or else swoon to death
and I awoke and found me here
on top of a chilly cloud in the sky.

120. Lucifer

Her whisper in my
ears bring out
the devil in me,
I hold her words
safe between my lip,
her soul makes them
speak of heaven.

121. Unresponsive

She loves the bit about whisky
and numbs his tongue with ice.

122. Stood still

We stood Poised,
she stroked my hair
but she hates me now
because I did not kiss.

123. The winged war

Encouraging a natural nocturnal
It's like herding a vampires unicorn
when the winged war is internal
begin to hold our breath
as our muscles clench rhythmically
this is a necessary and
a universal predecessor to orgasm
In the hands of an artist.

124. Aloof

I keep myself aloof
from the world
I hope you always
keep me close
my pen pleads with you
I want to see this world
through muse eyes.

125. Imagine,

the pattern of shadows
cast by the curvy body on a white wall,
dancing in a soft breeze
an electric-blue damselfly darts
from point to point on the wall,
now in moonlight,
now in the shade,
as though tracing
an invisible design.

126. Warbling

When she downward cast her eyes
a whale gasped on the floor,
When she raised her lustrous gaze
a beast peeped from the window,
When she turned away, her eyes
a pigeon perched on the sill,
My heart and mind warbling
with pathetic pleadings
fade not in haste.

127. Drizzle

Raindrops gently touch my chin
like the raindrops which touch
my chin and deceiving the land
you are falling on me
I take off the raincoat.

128. Glimpse

I drew my eyes closed,
she touched my chest
lightly with her fingertips,
cold night airbrushing
against my skin.
I shiver and frailty
I let her warm me up,
on my skin, her mouth is warm and moist
kissing the inside of my shirt
neck, chest, and chin
moving back up to my chest,
never stopping too long in any one spot.
I open my eyes for a second
and catch her glimpse at me
like she's waiting for me
to give herself.

129. Refuse

"Of course, I can't refuse"
When she opened her arms for a cuddle.

130. Wand

From whence has she got this fire
that burns when he withdraw
and cools when he approaches.

131. Ordinary

Look back on time with a kindly heart,
It's ordinary to love the beautiful
but it's beautiful to love the ordinary,
our blank is filled with beauty
She was doubtless with it.

132. carries

They come into the bookshop,
clutched hands with uneven steps.
they choose a few old books
she hands him her choices
he knows he'll be reading
some of the pages to her.
His hand guiding her,
to the door, He carries her books
he was an open book in her hand.

133. Destroy

She was ruthless lava
yet she was a reviving warm.
phoenix desire the things
which will destroy in the end
obtains new life by arising
from the ashes.

134. Enduring

His eyes looking into her eyes
were the indefinite continued,
progress of existence
and events in the past,
present, and future
regarded as a whole.

135. Umbrella

He was her device consisting of
a circular canopy of cloth
on a folding metal frame
supported by a central rod,
used as protection against rain,
sunlight and sometimes for
the kiss in the public garden.

136. Desserts

She is the round fruit of
a tree from the rose family,
which typically has
thin red skin and crisp flesh.
multiple varieties have been
developed as desserts
in the darkroom.

137. Learn

Want to feel witnesses in despair
In the absence of hope
where every butterfly is bold to go,
learn to Fly.

138. Belief

The sunsets and the moon
rises, again each day for her
the sun was her nature's west,
to the fair repose
where did she always hope?
there is a place between
moonsets & sunrises.

139. Feminine

The pair of eyes
that I've confused,
that seem to kill those
who look at them,
were in hostilities with
the feminine simplicity.

140. I don't know

Why does her all move towards His lips?

141. Statement

Fingerprints on everything
wine glass,
mug handles,
light switch,
and goosebumped skin.

142. Missing

My chores glimmer with new radiance
at the half-chance of being loved,
I would weave cloth for your shoulders
so that I could always be touching your skin.

143. And tell me,

In the open window,
the candle betrays the wind's summer breath
and the night settles down around us.
There are no limits to what may be given,
darkness simply lets down a curtain for that.
whispering in bed in unison to the words,
and tell me,
one more time.

144. Astronaut

The weight
of any object in the
the Center of the earth is
zero Like myself
within the boundaries of
your beauty.

145. The kingdom

I'll be the warrior
to fight for our love
we'll fly together,
fly higher than the cloud
I'll be your wall
and shield you from jeopardy,
I'll take all the pains,
to me, they are no strangers.
You'll be the queen
in the kingdom of my heart.

146. Feeble

Every time I hear
the echoes of your angelic voice
all other sounds vanished
even the smallest noise.
I don't know what I feel
I think I'm falling;
hanging at the edge
with hopes that someone is catching
my heart is too feebles.

147. Why

Why is she in my arms?
Why is she holding me?
Why is she kissing my face?
Why is she licking my neck?
Why is she hugging me?
Why is she feeding nectar to me?
Why this angel is so far away from heaven?
Why does God not come down and guide her back to heaven?
Whenever I surrender myself to you
I think to myself.

148. Pray

Let's hope
the closed eyes don't pray
Never to see beloved again
Because you are present
In every prayer of mine.

149. Tedious

The hard day,
tonight soak our lips in wine.

150. Invisible

She dried after her bath,
toweled underarms and legs,
a sound came from the other room,
cello sonatas, moan,
we listened,
she played with a pretend cello
drawing an invisible bow
across invisible strings,
she dried between thighs,
eyed her mirrored self,
plumpish, pink skin,
as the music slowed,
we head to one side
invisible cello,
kissing deep and passionate,
she closed her eyes,
the cello stilled,
invisible bow
blown away
like leaves in the wind.

151. Eternity

Her gaze is most precious
and sacred treasure
a girl whose beauty
knows no measure,
I can spend an eternity
just staring into her eyes
thanking the universe for
showing me her iris,
the most stunning being in
my universe.

152. I'm home

What I bring home to you
flowers,
poetry,
and the strawberries.

153. Possess

When her day was pillowed with tedious,
he was a rectangular cloth bag
stuffed with feathers,
is used to support her
head when she lay down.

154. Honey edge

He lipped at her palm
a dark handful, sweet-edged,
dissolving in one mouthful.
A fruity rub on the tongue
and the taste is promote
the little honey edge
ate wild strawberries out of
her hands for sweetness.

155. In brasserie,

He stared at another woman
she turns the knife in her hand slowly.

156. Now sing

This choir of socks,
shoes, shirts, skirts,
undergarments
as the day declined.
The Unasked Haiku,
she brought out her breasts,
to be caressed
no wonder I too
now sing all night.

157. Remaining

*Only the soft substance
consisting of muscle
and fat that is found between
the skin and bones
remains what it was meant to be,*

158. Silence

The silence spoke to the star
the star to silence was wed
and the moon was a priest that day
and they made their bridal bed
high in the galaxy,
He hung breathless on her breath
speechless, who listened well
could not speak or think or wish
till silence broke the spell
the white star had heard
her silent lover's moaned,

159. I swear

My sunflower garden
has no strong aroma
I sent thee a sunflower plant,
it could not be withered
when being my sunflowers are
breathed your breath
and you sent it back to me
since when it grows,
they spread scent
I swear.

160. Grey blankets

The sky winter cries
clouds frozen tears
wind blows
unseen flutes
here is the zone for leisure
at the beneath of her neck,

161. Quivers

My illusion was never created
something like you
How is it that you are real?
Why is it that my heart still skips a beat,
every time I feel your touch?
You make my heart beat fast,
You make my knees quiver,
you are the sexiest girl I know
Loving you is splendor,
I need your touch,
I will never let you go.

162. Limits in joy

We aligned mouths
we entwined,
the forest is the abode of life,
and were the days
gathered in my laughing gear,
little flute of a reed
hast carried over hills and valleys,
and hast breathed through
Its melodies were eternally new
At the immortal touch of your hands,
my little heart loses its limits in joy
and gives birth to utterance ineffable.

163. Draw

My fingers feel the warmth of a fire
when you draw it on
my body with your blush,
and with a brush like a finger
let's paint our love
let's lit up the fire.

164. The same song

Heart,
beats your name
right down to the core,
Filling me with such joy
and so much more,
your shoulders are so warm,
I just can't take my head away,
here in my arms is where you belong,
our two hearts beating
to the same song.

165. You will

Rose leaves the petals
when the rose is dead
are heaped for the beloved's bed
and so your thoughts
my eyes wait for alert,
with strained delight
eyelashes are hate to close
as though they knew that
you will come to me
before the sunrise,

166. Dawn

Love birds own the day
Lust bats own the night
at the break of dawn
both take flight,
until darkness is gone
vampire bats steal our lust blood
empire birds heal our love
want them to stay in their soul,
by the nightly game
will shift into bats.

167. Linger

Life's purposes
and my ambition,
the blue eyes
that meet the brown eyes in a dream
the brown eyes from so eastern
and the blue eyes from the west,
blue that catches the early
light of days yet to be met
and fall and meet again, then linger
time and distance are all forgotten for a little while
blue eyes shut brown eyes with a kiss
those are dim and ride away to sleep
life's purposes and my ambition are blind.

168. Spectators

She kisses him
The cafe applauds

169. Prove

Shall I forget the face of a bright moonlight?
Whose beauty is comparable to you;
Shall I not recall the way your hair dances in the summer air?
And how your gaze warms my cold winter;
Shall I hold your chin and will forever yearn for it?
I long for the day when our tongues would meet;
Shall I pass a day without seeing you?
Shall I live another day without saying how much I miss you?
Or miss a chance to prove my feelings are fantasy.

170. Alcohol-abuser

Your eyes,
touch,
lips,
soul,
presence
Mesmerize and entangle me
completely like a boozer.

171. Extirpate

My fire of love in youthful blood
like what is provoked in brushwood,
born in the hour of glee and warmth
with warmth and glee may perish,
but for moment burns yet at
that moment makes a mighty noise
It crackles the sulfur of sorrow
turns soon itself destroys.

172. Perhaps

What if
there was a moon
with blue trees
What if
there was a planet
full of rainbows
What if
there was a comet
with a butterfly farm
These things are
happening in my mind
when I place my lips
beneath your neck.

173. The tune

Ms. Piano girl, how your
fingers rain down on the keys,
the keys were not something to be seeing
it was just a matter of using some feeling.
let it rain in this dark sky
let the storm hammer the strings
let's drench in the tune of
our seducing love drops.

174. Before the sun

Know I think of you every day
I hope that you do the same.

175. Lens

My eyes were in a trance.
Through the camera lens
she appears to me
but in negative
she looks so differently,
Delicious in curve
shadows of black
enhanced is her shape
negative shadows
Through the camera lens
she appears to be
the negative
of what I mostly see.

176. Wrote

The scent of your hair
the vividness of your eyelashes
the curve of your lips
this all the little things
that makes me stop and stare,
let me sing to you all the songs I wrote
til you sleep in my embrace,
and I'll keep you safe
and warm until the
sunlight kisses your face.

177. Song of heart

Every heart has a melody to sing
Incomplete until another heart
whispers back,
I can sing the song of our heart
through my silence
at the palm print of yours
in my chest.

178. Once I read,

Heaven's angels use
white robes to take a bath,
but this angle from an evil spirit
what you need clothes than my skin
full nakedness, all joys are due to you,
license my roving hands, and let them go
before, behind, between above, below
as souls are bodiless, bodies unclothed
must be to taste whole joys of body.

179. Gazed

She blushed with lusty love,
She half enclosed me with her arms
pressed me with a meek embrace,
I felt her breath on my neck
I calmed her fears and tears
and she was calm
and bending back her head, looked up
and gazed upon my face
I take a sip of eternity.

180. After the sun

My night has become meaningless
in muse absence
I have a request,
please come only once
and know my
unsaid feelings.

181. Measure

She was a device for measuring time,
indicating hours, minutes,
and sometimes seconds,
typically by his hands
on her dial.

182. Moonless

*A condition of body and mind
that typically recurs for several
hours every night.*

183. Hold

He folds into the dent of her chest,
The crook of her shoulder.
Hold this moment
before we open our bodies,
"Don't move,"
"not now"
"let's be still,"
She whispered.

184. Stop and stare

What is that I hear?
It is not your conversation
that does not keep me entertained
but, rather the way you look at me
that makes me feel sustained
It's the curve of your lips
and the curl of your long hair
It's all of the little things
that makes my mind
stop and stare
What is that I hear?
That note was just a kiss.

185. Fidgety

All facts of anxious eye contact
the attack and,
the interlock Of tongues,
the charms of arms
shook at her hug of her,
closed on it tight as could.
The upright warmth of her belly
lay all along with mine
glued together for a minute.

186. Conquer

If my love for you
is in every grain of sand,
all of the beaches will
assuredly run out of land.
The land to be its shore
and the sea will dominate
with the waves of love,
There is a person right
inside of me who's deeply
in love with you.
A person who
would sail any sea, all of that
he would do, just for you.
He's not afraid of anything
completely nothing at all,
because for you
he will conquer all his fears
to save you from all those tears.

187. Otherwise

You are that rainbow of color
when my sky has
turned gray.
You are the smile
that I need when I've had
a crummy day.
You are the one
I feel at peace with
when I'm lying in your chest
You are the candle's flame
in a room otherwise
dark.

188. Garden jasmine

When from the bed, she woke
clothed from neck to knee
stitched from cloud
In her white night skirt
pretty she seems
like garden jasmine,
pure from the night and
perfect for the day.

189. As I lay on my terrace

I'm not lonely,
I just miss you
not being there.
I see your face in
the stars at night,
I close my eyes and
hold you tight.
It's not being alone, I fear,
I'm not lonely.
I just miss you
As I lay on my terrace.

190. seen

They turn to leave the cafe,
he tucked her scarf around
against the anticipated sunlight.

191. Her heart is,

The expanse of water covers
most of the earth's surface
and surrounds its landmasses,
he is the thief of pearls in her sea.

192. Illuminated

What the moon saw.
The moon is lying in the pool,
quite still
I offer it a toe,
which it licks,
shivering just a little,
I could choose to stay outside
rather, I decided to slip in
my darkness is washed
in her moonlight.

193. Wakes and wed

When the sky turns gray,
when the star twinkles,
the blue moon wakes and weds her
in the blue through the window
powerless to speak
about my blue dreams.
The winds are enticed by Maiden
I take a breather for her
as listen to her heartbeat
she is the only star
that dies not with the dark.

194. Ink

My diary speaks a lot
of my dream about you
that try to express a lot
from the margins of the paper
to the doors of the sky
till the depth of the ocean.
In the romancing moonlight,
you and me
holding each other
as the fragrance of you
until the sunrise
snowy mountains
to the cold breeze,
An unfixed colorful clouds
and even from rain to rainbow
all this is possible With
the nip of my pen
that depicts my heart
by the ink of you.

195. Perceive with the eyes

We all had seen that scene,
While someone secretly has romance.

196. That day

At a waterfall
You and me
exchange kisses
under the shade of
a nameless tree for us,
I exclaim
how excited I am
and we are without
a camera or canvas,
I pen her sugared lips and
writing today by recalling.

197. Hide

I must hide no more,
my heart glows housing the smile
you cause me to make it
is this nervousness that I must break
these hidden feelings
I must hide no more,
As I walk up the path that leads to your door
ringing the bell hearing the jow.

198. There is magic in theatre

It can't be understood
the dim lights and smell of your hair,
Is an illness I suffer happily
it's dizziness that seated with me
it's a place between your two-hand,
Your shoulder is a special place
it excites me to no end.
I hear your whispers on my neck
Shhhhh....sweetheart, the film is ending.

199. He loved her

Against promise,
Against peace,
Against happiness,
Against hope,
Against reason,
He loved her.

200. Never once had I played the guitar

Never once had I placed the guitar on my lap.
You drew me in
with your tunes of promise
you tempted my loneliness
with a single flick of a string,
When I drown grief
your music was my lullaby
the sound of your tune,
no matter how made up it was,
Even in this crowded world
and the panics of my heart
you wrapped yourself around me.

201. Perceive

Faint the night wind blew,
heaves the grasses
whence you wilt never rise
is of the air that passes
and knows not if it sighs.

202. You called for my hand

And there we were
hand in hand,
Even though it was a game
I don't think I could ever feel the same,
Close my eyes, brush my lips,
stand nice and tall, and you hold my hips.
It was right next to mine
our bodies pressed together, yet we stayed
silent as a mime.
Open my eyes to find the surprise
that you upon me.

203. Endeavor

If there is any magic in the world,
it boldest be an attempt of
understanding love.

204. The moon appears bluish

A phenomenon whereby
the moon appears bluish
and the stars deny their beams,
When I am in thy
low mound on the thee,
It has a simple gravity I do not understand!

205. It was many years ago,

A beauty you were born.
You are the girl who was unique
and beloved by all
and even the angels wished
to know your fate,
You deserve a crown
a scepter, a throne
your grin is so breathtaking,
my love is for you alone.
There is nothing I would rather do
then spend all of my time makings
a queen out of you.

206. Yeah I heard

Love stories delightful,
Whenever it is the subject of a rumor.

207. Soaring

The thought of kissing you
it's stuck in my heart,
your chin is bright and warm
shining through the darkest storm.
Your eyes sparkle like
stars in the night sky
when I stare into them
I feel like I am soaring high
to paradise.

208. Music and muse

The eyes closed,
the postural muscles relaxed,
and overthinking was practically suspended
the nervous system is relatively hyperactive.

209. Without your breath

cannot live.
I need your lips on mine,
nothing at all I wouldn't give.
Thoughts of you surround me,
you're the pounding of my heart.
The love you give defines me,
my existence is no longer dark.

210. When she smiled

The edges of her cheeks dissolved
into a thousand wrinkles,
and her wide brown eyes reflected the sun.

211. A minute

The hug that scorched
the desert dunes to glass
and sealed the sun in its frozen,
I should have kissed her
if the hail had lasted a minute more.

212. At midnight

As she saw another train sail By,
She waited, Nervously at the station.
The hissing drift of winter rain,
water dripping From great flanged wheels.
She was too blind in the rain.
and doubt to speak, but reached
from the platform until our chilled hands met.

213. Your hair upon my shoulders

Falling like water over boulders.
Collarbones have great potential.
They are essential,
for the cost of my effectiveness
the way lips disclose,
The neat arrangement of your teeth,
Half above and half beneath In rows
all legendary obstacles lay between us.

214. Theory

As a newton's apple falls from a branch,
he is falling toward her, fallen.
moving slowly,
pussyfoot, as excitedly
as a kitten towards milk.

215. Doorstep

The sun denies the beams,
When you Come not at my door to knock.

216. Close

I cannot open you
like a newspaper, but
you put me down
like a newspaper.
Never close your lips to those
whom you have already
opened your heart.

217. As they stayed in,

Freestanding bathtub
the tang of her waist he handled,
and chase the soap for an hour.
They heard the sound of rain
above them calling dizzying
faint as the triangle drops turned.

218. Located in her lap

My scalp on her fingertips.
The induction of a state of
consciousness in myself.
Apparently loses the power
of voluntary action
and is highly responsive to
her suggestion and direction.

219. Capacity

She has the ability to understand his Iris move immediately, without the need for conscious reasoning.

220. Insomnia

Her series of thoughts,
voice, images, and sensations
occurring in my mind during sleep.

221. Butterflies

Positive transformations,
hope during a dark time,
and new beginnings.

222. End

Where dark ends, love begins.
Where love ends, poetry begins.